Germany

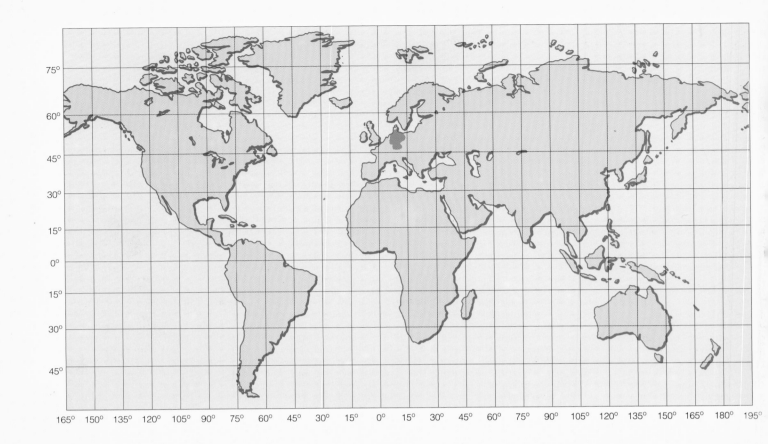

Germany

David Flint

RAINTREE STECK-VAUGHN
P U B L I S H E R S

Austin, Texas

Copyright Permissions,
Steck-Vaughn Company,
P.O.Box 26015,
Austin, TX 78755
Published by Raintree Steck-Vaughn Publishers, an imprint of
Steck-Vaughn Company

Design Roger Kohn
Consultant David Burtenshaw,
Principal Lecturer in
Geography
Editors Penny Clarke, Helene Resky
DTP editor Helen Swansbourne
Picture research Valerie Mulcahy
Illustration János Márffy

We are grateful to the following for permission
to reproduce photographs:
Front cover: Kaiser Wilhelm I Church, Berlin, Telegraph Colour
Library and Gisela Floto for children photograph; Camera
Press, page 8 (Jonathan Haddock); J. Allan Cash, page 17;
Robert Harding Picture Library, pages 15, 21, 29, 31, 36; The
Image Bank, pages 35 (Gary Cralle), 38 (Hans Wolf); Magnum
Photos, page 39 (James Nachtwey); Marco Polo, page 42 (F.
Bouillot); Picturepoint, page 18 (Dr. Reinbacher); Rex
Features, pages 19 (Cham), 25 *above* (Boccon Glbod), 25
below (François Lehr); Carolina Salguero/Odyssey/TRIP, page
20; Select, page 23 (Dirk Robbers); Spectrum Colour Library,
pages 8/9 (J. Raga), 34; Tony Stone Worldwide, pages 10, 11
(Manfred Mehlig), 22, 33, 40, 41 (Charles Thatcher); Zefa,
pages 12 (Rossenbach), 13 (Sharp Shooters), 14 (J. Pfaff), 16
(F. Damm), 27 (F. Damm), 28, 30 (Streichan), 32 (Justitz), 37
(Streichan), 43.

The statistics given in this book are the most up-to-date
available at the time of going to press

Printed and bound in Hong Kong by
Paramount Printing Group Ltd

1 2 3 4 5 6 7 8 9 0 HK 99 98 97 96 95 94

Library of Congress Cataloging-in-Publication Data
Flint, David, 1946—
Germany / David Flint.
p. cm. — (Country Fact Files)
Includes biographical references and index.
Summary: Examines the landscape, climate, weather,
population, culture, and industries of Germany.
ISBN 0-8114-1845-6
1. Germany – Juvenile literature. [1. Germany.]
I. Title. II. Series. DD17.F55 1993a
943—dc20
93-26543
CIP AC

Words that are explained in the glossary are printed in SMALL CAPITALS the first time they are mentioned in the text.

INTRODUCTION

Germany is a large, powerful, and important country. It has close links with its neighbors and is a leading member of the group of countries that make up the European Community (EC). Germany is at the heart of Europe, stretching 495 miles (800 km) from the Baltic coast in the north to the Austrian border in the south. From the Polish border in the east it stretches 435 miles (700 km) west to the Netherlands.

Germany has not always been a large, united country. For much of its early history, it was made up of many small separate independent states, each with its own ruling family. In 1871 Bismarck, the German chancellor, united all these states into the German Empire. Between 1914 and 1945, Germany fought and lost two world wars. Germany supported Austria against Russia in 1914, and this led to World War I. The U.S., France, Great Britain, and Russia finally won this conflict in 1918.

In 1933 Adolf Hitler and the Nazi party came to power in Germany. Hitler built up a powerful army, navy, and air force with which to conquer Europe. In 1939 Germany invaded Poland, starting World War II. Germany was finally defeated by the U.S., Great Britain, and the Soviet Union in 1945.

◀ The Berlin Wall symbolized Germany's division into two countries: East Germany and West Germany. It was finally demolished in 1990.

As a result of that defeat, Germany became divided into two countries: East Germany and West Germany. These developed separately, with their own governments. East Germany had a communist government while West Germany was a Western-style democracy. By 1989, people in East Germany had decided they wanted a different form of government. There were marches and protests that forced the government to make changes. Finally, in October 1990, the two Germanys were reunited.

GERMANY AT A GLANCE

- Area: 137,838 square miles (375,000 sq km)
- Population: 79.15 million
- Density: 577 people per square mile (221 people per sq km)
- Capital: Berlin, population 3.1 million
- Other main cities: Hamburg 1.5 million, Munich 1.2 million, Cologne 946,000
- Highest mountain: Zugspitze 9,720 feet (2,963 m)
- Language: German
- Main religion: Christianity
- Currency: Deutschmark, written as DM. One deutschmark is divided into 100 pfennigs
- Economy: Highly industrialized
- Major resources: Coal, brown coal (LIGNITE), timber
- Major products: Automobiles, machinery, engineering goods, electrical and electronic goods
- Environment: Much pollution of forests in the west and rivers and lakes, especially near eastern industrial centers

◀ *The Brandenburg Gate was the busiest crossroads in Europe before 1939. Then it became the dividing line between East and West. Now, once again, it bustles with life.*

THE LANDSCAPE

Germany is a country of broad plains, thick forests, deep valleys, and high mountains. The highest mountain peaks are in the Alps or the Erzgebirge (Ore Mountains) of southern Germany. The thick forests covering the mountains' lower slopes give way to meadows. Many flowers, such as the blue gentian, used to be found in these meadows, but their numbers have been reduced by farmers using artificial fertilizers and PESTICIDES. Higher up the meadows give way to bare rocky slopes, covered with ice at the very highest levels.

Central Germany has high plains, valleys, and forests. The Rhine and Elbe rivers carve their way across the region, providing routes for main roads and railroads.

In the past most of Germany was covered by forests of birch, beech, and oak. Much of this woodland has been cut down for farms, towns, and factories, but there are still important woodland areas, such as the Black Forest.

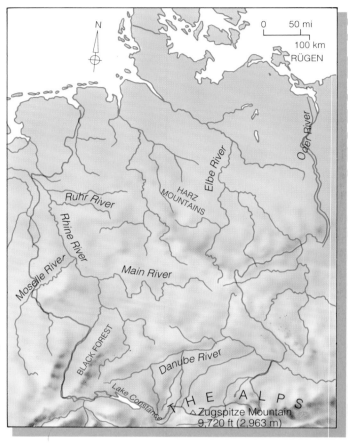

◄ **High mountains, with glaciers and waterfalls, make the German Alps a popular tourist area all year round.**

▲ **The river systems that flow from Germany's mountains and across the country's wide plains have always been an important means of transportation and communication across Europe.**

In the last hundred years many of the areas of natural forest have been replanted with faster growing coniferous trees like pine, fir, and spruce. More than half the country's forests have been planted in this way, especially in the south and east.

The Rhine River is one of Germany's most important waterways. It links northern and southern Europe and is used by thousands of barges transporting goods.

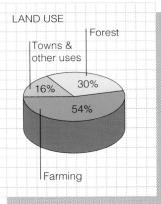

LAND USE

Forest

Towns & other uses

16%

30%

54%

Farming

North Germany is an area of low hills, flat plains, shallow lakes, and marshes. On the Baltic coast there are long stretches of fine sand popular with summer vacationers. Rügen is a low chalk island in the Baltic Sea separated from the mainland by a narrow channel.

KEY FACTS ON RIVERS

● The Rhine River flows north and west and is 818 miles (1,320 km) long.
● The Elbe River, an important river flowing from southeast to the northwest, is 724 miles (1,167 km) long.
● The Danube River rises in southwest Germany and flows 798 miles (1,287 km) east through seven other countries to the Black Sea.

KEY FACTS ON LAKES

● Lake Constance: 334 square miles (538.5 sq km)
● Lake Müritz: 71 square miles (115.3 sq km)
● Lake Chiem: 51 square miles (82 sq km)
● Lake Schwerin: 41 square miles (65.5 sq km)

CLIMATE AND WEATHER

Climatically Germany is in a location in Europe where the warm, wet conditions coming from the west meet the colder, drier conditions coming from the east. Because of this, the climate and weather varies from year to year. In some years winters are bitterly cold and dry, while in other years milder, wetter winters can be expected.

In general, southern Germany is warmer for most of the year than the north. However, this general pattern is influenced by altitude. Over much of the country people live and work in areas that are more than 1,475 feet (450 m) above sea level. Temperatures fall by 1°F for every 272 feet (1°C for every 150 m) of altitude. This means that places on the Rhine plateau, for example, are 5.4°F (3°C) to 7.2°F (4°C) colder than nearby Cologne. Higher areas also tend to have heavier rain, and snow

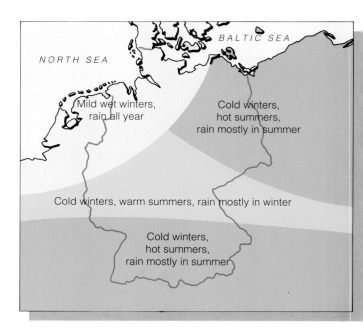

▲ **East and south Germany have colder winters but warmer summers than the north and west.**

▼ **Hamburg's rain falls all year round but Berlin gets mo. of its rain in the summer months.**

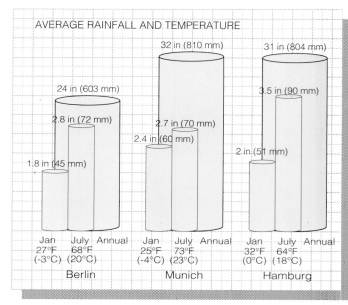

AVERAGE RAINFALL AND TEMPERATURE

	Berlin			Munich			Hamburg		
Annual			24 in (603 mm)			32 in (810 mm)			31 in (804 mm)
July		2.8 in (72 mm)			2.7 in (70 mm)			3.5 in (90 mm)	
Jan	1.8 in (45 mm)			2.4 in (60 mm)			2 in (51 mm)		

Jan 27°F (-3°C)	July 68°F (20°C)	Annual	Jan 25°F (-4°C)	July 73°F (23°C)	Annual	Jan 32°F (0°C)	July 64°F (18°C)	Annual
Berlin			Munich			Hamburg		

◄ **Hot, sunny summers allow both red and white grapes to ripen even in central parts of the country. German wine is famous all over the world.**

falls throughout the year. This is because rainfall increases when rain-bearing winds are forced to rise over highland areas like the Black Forest.

Northern and western parts of Germany are affected by the moderating influence of the ocean. The ocean tends to make winters milder and summers cooler than places farther inland. As a result, the central and eastern regions, unaffected by the influence of the ocean, have cold winters but hot summers. These central and eastern areas also have a shorter growing season and more days with frost each year: Cologne has 44 frost days, but in contrast Berlin has 90.

▼ *Cold, snowy winters provide perfect conditions for the many Germans who are avid skiers. Cross-country skiing (called* LANGLAUF*) is popular with people of all ages.*

KEY FACTS

● Western parts of Germany receive 4 inches (100 mm) more rain a year than the eastern parts.
● Rainfall varies according to position. Places like Koblenz in the Rhine valley have 39 inches (1,000 mm) less rainfall a year than the surrounding hills.
● In the Rhine valley apple trees start to flower about April 20, but in Berlin, where it is colder, they do not start until after May 9.

NATURAL RESOURCES

The economic growth of Germany since 1945 has been based on energy from coal, oil, gas, and nuclear power. Germany has both black coal and brown coal (lignite). The largest black coalfield is the Ruhr in the western part of the country. The Ruhr provided the power for German industries and towns throughout the 19th century, and it is still important. The early coal mines were in the southern part of the field where the coal was found on the surface. Now mining is concentrated in deep mines in the north of the coalfield.

Lignite, is extracted from huge STRIP MINES. Most lignite is burned in power stations.

Germany has no oil, so this fuel has to be imported. Some comes by pipeline from Russia and the North Sea. The rest is imported from the Middle East and South America (the OPEC countries), and comes by barge and pipeline via the port of Rotterdam in the Netherlands. About 60 percent of Germany's natural gas is imported from the Netherlands and the North Sea. The rest comes from the Middle East and Siberia in Russia.

Many nuclear power stations were built during the last 20 years. The aim was to reduce Germany's dependence on imported fuels such as oil and natural gas. However nuclear power stations are very expensive to build, and the public is concerned about the dangers of an accidental release of radioactivity. Disposing of the radioactive waste from these power stations is also a problem. As a result, Germany has stopped building nuclear power stations. Five reactors were reported shut down in 1990.

Hydroelectricity is an important source of power in parts of southern Germany, where there are fast-flowing rivers.

▼ **Strip brown coal mining is much cheaper than deep coal mining but can do great damage to the environment.**

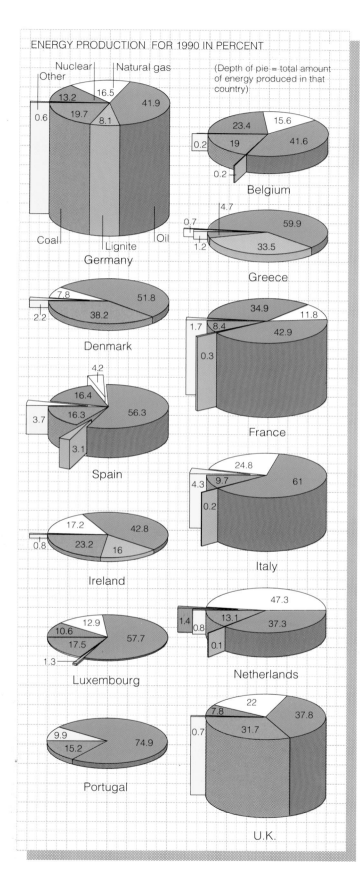

ENERGY PRODUCTION FOR 1990 IN PERCENT

Germany
Other
Nuclear | Natural gas
13.2 | 16.5
0.6 | 19.7 | 8.1 | 41.9
Coal | Lignite | Oil

(Depth of pie = total amount of energy produced in that country)

Belgium
15.6
23.4
41.6
0.2 | 19
0.2

Greece
4.7
0.7 | 59.9
1.2 | 33.5

Denmark
7.8 | 51.8
2.2 | 38.2

France
34.9 | 11.8
1.7 | 8.4 | 42.9
0.3

Spain
4.2
16.4
3.7 | 16.3 | 56.3
3.1

Ireland
17.2 | 42.8
0.8 | 23.2 | 16

Italy
24.8
4.3 | 9.7 | 61
0.2

Luxembourg
12.9
10.6
17.5 | 57.7
1.3

Netherlands
47.3
1.4 | 0.8 | 13.1 | 37.3
0.1

Portugal
9.9
15.2 | 74.9

U.K.
22
7.8 | 37.8
0.7 | 31.7

KEY FACTS

● In 1990 Germany produced more than 12 million tons of brown coal (lignite), making it the world's largest producer.
● Black coal production averages 77 million tons a year.
● There were 300,000 coal miners in 1960 but only 103,000 in 1990.

Hydroelectric power stations are expensive to build but cheap to run because the fuel (water) is free. Germany is also experimenting with generating power from the wind and the sun.

Germany's forests are another important resource. More than a million trees are cut down every year for furniture, papermaking, or house-building. The government encourages forest owners to plant more trees than they fell.

▼ *Germany is experimenting with wind power. This is an important form of* RENEWABLE ENERGY.

POPULATION

◀ **About 60 percent of Germans live in main cities. During World War II, many towns and cities were badly damaged, but these have been carefully rebuilt.**

▼ **Hamburg, Berlin, and Munich are Germany's largest cities with populations of more than one million.**

After Germany was unified in 1871, the country's population grew by more than a million each year until 1912. By 1939, Germany had a population of 43 million. After World War II, the country was divided into two states, and the city of Berlin was also divided. The area of Germany controlled by the Russian forces became East Germany, with East Berlin as its capital. The area controlled by the Allies (the U.S., Great Britain, and France)

KEY FACTS

● Population (in millions)
1989 West Germany 64.17
       East Germany 16.4
1990 United Germany 78.5
1991 United Germany 79.5
1990 Annual average income per person $14,600. (The average income per person in the U.S. is $23,150)
1990 577 people per square mile (221 per sq km)
● 1990 Religions (percent)
Christianity 91 (Protestant 65; Catholic 26)
Other 9

0   50 mi
100 km

□ Hamburg
● Bremen
▲ Hanover   ■ Berlin
▲ Magdeburg
● Dortmund   Halle ●   ● Leipzig
● Düsseldorf
● Cologne   Jena ●   Dresden ●
● Frankfurt
▲ Mannheim   ▲ Nuremberg
● Stuttgart
Munich □

■ More than 2 million
□ 1–2 million
● 500,000–1million
▲ 200,000–500,000

▶ *The country-side is a very important part of German life, both for producing food and as a place for recreation.*

became West Germany, with Bonn as its capital. West Berlin, although surrounded by East Germany, was a part of West Germany.

The movement of people and goods between the two parts of the country became very difficult. Large numbers of East Germans disliked the new communist state and fled to West Germany. Many of these refugees were doctors, teachers, health care workers, scientists, and other people vital to East Germany. So, on August 13, 1961, the

East Germans built the Berlin Wall to keep people from escaping to the West. The whole frontier between the two countries was lined, on the East German side by barbed wire and watchtowers, and guarded by armed soldiers with fierce dogs.

Despite these measures East Germany's population declined as people still found ways to escape. Between 1961 and 1989, 74 people were killed trying to escape from East to West Berlin. In contrast West Germany's population grew as the country's economy boomed.

Since reunification in 1990, Germany's population has continued to grow, but the rate of increase is slowing. People are also living longer thanks to advances in medicine. This means there will be an increasing number of old people who will need to be cared for in the future.

◀ *Communist East Germany's population declined by 1.6 million between 1950 and 1989, but West Germany's grew by more than 10 million.*

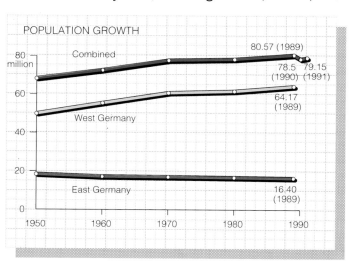

POPULATION GROWTH

80 million
Combined
80.57 (1989)
78.5   79.15
(1990) (1991)

60
West Germany
64.17 (1989)

40

20
East Germany
16.40 (1989)

0
1950   1960   1970   1980   1990

Some people in Germany are leaving towns to live in villages in the nearby countryside. They feel that rural areas offer more peace and quiet with less pollution and a better quality of life. So farms in villages close to towns are bought by city dwellers who divide and sell the land and often redesign the buildings. During weekdays, these villages are very quiet when everyone has gone to work, and life only revives in the evening, when people return.

People in Germany are also concerned about the issue of FOREIGN WORKERS in their country. Throughout the 1960s and 1970s, German economic growth was rapid. One result of this was that people from the poorer countries of Europe, such as Turkey and Portugal, moved to Germany in search of better paying jobs. Many Germans did not want to do the dirtier, unskilled, often dangerous jobs such as refuse disposal. At this time, the foreign workers were made welcome. Usually, just one person from a family moved to Germany, then after a few years other family members joined him or her

The problem has not been helped by German reunification. The problems of integrating the bustling, prosperous western part of the country with the much poorer, run-down eastern part are enormous.

Today, the country's economic growth is slower, and many Germans have lost their jobs. These unemployed people often resent foreign workers who, they feel, are stealing their jobs. Foreign workers usually live in big cities, where they keep their own language, culture, and religion. Their life-style is different from that of local people. In some places this has created social tensions. High concentrations of foreign workers can make local people feel outnumbered. For example 70 percent of all pupils in Frankfurt's primary

▲ **With a growing elderly population treatments using spa water are becoming increasingly popular.**

▼ **German villages have fewer farms than 20 years ago. For more and more people, farming is only a secondary occupation.**

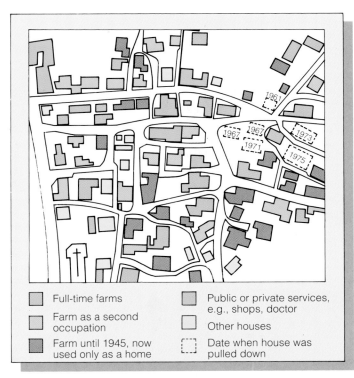

■ Full-time farms	■ Public or private services, e.g., shops, doctor
□ Farm as a second occupation	□ Other houses
■ Farm until 1945, now used only as a home	⬚ Date when house was pulled down

schools are from the families of foreign workers.

Life is not easy for foreign workers. Many cannot afford the fare to visit relatives, so feelings of homesickness are common. Demonstrations against these workers can lead to violence, and some people are trying to persuade some of them to return home.

KEY FACTS

● Ten million people fled from East to West Germany between 1945 and 1991.
● Two million foreign workers live in Germany. Together with their families they make a total of 4.5 million people.
● Percentage of total population in age groups

Under 6	6
6 to 14	9
15 to 24	15
25 to 44	29
45 to 64	26
65 and over	15

● Life expectancy

Men	72.1 years
Women	78.7 years

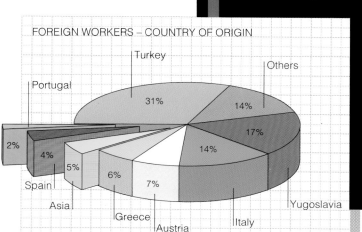

FOREIGN WORKERS – COUNTRY OF ORIGIN

Turkey 31%
Others 14%
Yugoslavia 17%
Italy 14%
Austria 7%
Greece 6%
Asia 5%
Spain 4%
Portugal 2%

▶ *Most of Germany's foreign workers come from the poorer countries of southern Europe.*

▶ *Foreign workers came mainly to do the jobs that Germans were un-willing to do. Now that unemployment among German people has increased, foreign workers have become unpopular because German workers feel that jobs should be reserved for Germans.*

Children usually attend kindergartens or nursery schools when they are three years old. Germany was the first country to introduce schooling for young children, but the system has now spread to many other countries. Some nursery schools are free, but in others parents have to pay. Children start primary school when they are six. When they are ten, they go to a GYMNASIUM (grammar school), a REALSCHULE (middle school), or HAUPTSCHULE (secondary school). Each type of school provides general education and training, though the Hauptschule and Realschule tend to concentrate on technical skills. At 18, students who want to go to a university take an exam called the ARBITUR.

The school day starts at 7:30 A.M. in summer and 8 A.M. in winter and ends in the early afternoon. Then students go home for lunch. There is a mid-morning break of about 30 minutes when children eat the sandwiches they have brought. This is called the "second breakfast." Usually there are lessons on Saturday mornings.

Workers in Germany's factories and offices now have at least four weeks paid vacation each year. Until the 1970s, people worked a 40-hour week, but now a 36-hour week is quite common. As a result, people have more free time for their leisure activities.

Germans enjoy both watching and taking part in many sports, from soccer to sailing, skiing, and cycling. Many towns have fitness trails (*Trimmdich-pfade*) in parks and wooded areas. Soccer is the most popular spectator sport, followed by gymnastics. Special classes in sports help pupils develop their skills from an early age.

▶ *The different types of school in Germany.*

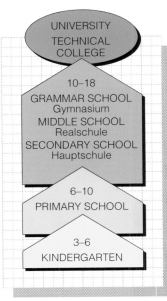

UNIVERSITY TECHNICAL COLLEGE
10–18 GRAMMAR SCHOOL Gymnasium MIDDLE SCHOOL Realschule SECONDARY SCHOOL Hauptschule
6–10 PRIMARY SCHOOL
3–6 KINDERGARTEN

▼ *Science and technology take up 15 percent of the school curriculum. Science fairs like this one are popular with all ages.*

KEY FACTS

● Between 1970 and 1990, the number of schoolchildren in West Germany fell by 2 million to 8.8 million. In East Germany the number of schoolchildren decreased by 800,000 to 2.5 million.

● The literacy rate is 99 percent.

● The most frequent cause of death in Germany in 1991 was heart attacks, followed by cancer.

▼ *Soccer is the most popular spectator sport in Germany, and more than 200,000 people attend a match each weekend. There were great celebrations throughout the country when Germany won the World Cup in 1990.*

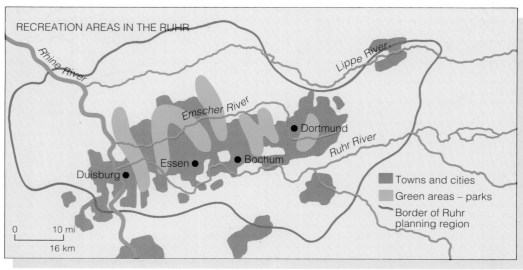

RECREATION AREAS IN THE RUHR

Rhine River

Lippe River

Emscher River

● Dortmund

Ruhr River

Essen ●   ● Bochum

Duisburg ●

■ Towns and cities
■ Green areas – parks
□ Border of Ruhr planning region

0   10 mi
16 km

◄ *An important industrial area, the Ruhr is one of the most densely populated parts of Germany. To improve the region, green areas have been created to separate the towns and cities, and more than 27 million trees have been planted.*

There are many festivals and celebrations throughout the year in Germany. Many of these festivals date back to pre-Christian or medieval times. Particular parts of the country are famous for their festivals, for example the *Oktoberfest* in Munich. During September, many villages and towns in the wine-making areas celebrate a good harvest with their WEINFEST. A new holiday or festival, celebrating the reunification of the country, is held on October 3. Easter is an important festival and on Easter Sunday children search their yards for Easter eggs hidden by their parents.

Germans are great readers, perhaps because printing was invented in

▲ The Beer Hall is crammed during the famous Munich Beer Festival held in October each year. Thousands of people from many parts of the world travel to Munich to take part in the Oktoberfest.

Germany in the 15th century. At least 10 percent of all books published in the world are written in German, which is also an important language for papers on scientific research.

Germany's two national television companies provide three channels. Channels One and Two are for national programs, while Channel Three covers local issues. Cable and satellite television are becoming increasingly common.

DAILY LIFE STATISTICS	1970	1980	1990*
1970 and 1980 figures for W. Germany			
1990 figures for united Germany			
Theaters			
No. of public theaters	194	221	410
No. of people attending	17.6mil	17.3mil	21.4mil
Movie theaters			
Number of movie theaters	3,597	3,354	4,127
Book publishing			
First editions published	38,703	54,572	60,175
Newspapers			
No. of newspapers	375	368	397
No. of magazines	5,142	6,243	8,197
Youth hostels			
No. of hostels	633	566	604
Sports associations			
No. of sports clubs	39,201	53,451	75,652
Club members	8.3mil	14.4mil	21.3mil

▼ *This newstand in Berlin is typical of many throughout the country. It sells a wide range of newspapers and magazines.*

KEY FACTS

● Every day the German people buy 30 million newspapers.
● The tabloid newspaper *Bild Zeitung* is read by more than 7 million people a day.
● Seventy percent of Germans have their daily newspaper delivered.
● Some famous newspapers are based in one city, like the *Hamburger Abendblatt* and *Frankfurter Allgemeine Zeitung*.
● The festival of *Karneval*, or *Fasching* as it is called in southern Germany, takes place on the three days before Ash Wednesday. There are street parties, costume competitions, and parades.

═RULES AND LAWS

Germany has a federal system of government very similar to the U.S. The country is divided into 16 LAENDER, or states, that have a great deal of power in their areas. People in the different Laender have strong feelings of independence and local identity. For example, people in the south often refer to themselves as Bavarians first and Germans second.

In Germany, like the U.S., people can vote from the age of 18. During elections, everyone has two votes. One is for a local candidate to represent them in the regional Laender government. The other is for a candidate from a national political party to represent them in the BUNDESTAG, the German equivalent of the U.S. Congress and the British House of Commons.

Members of each Laender government appoint members to represent them and their state in the BUNDESRAT. This is the upper house of the German parliament, and similar to the House of Representatives in the U.S. and the House of Lords in the U.K. It looks very closely at laws passed by the Bundestag.

▶ *Germany is divided into 16 Laender, or regional states. These vary greatly in size, number of cities, population, and degree of industrialization.*

KEY FACTS

● Germans regard voting as an important duty, and more than 80 percent register their choice in national and local elections.
● Political power is divided between the central government and the Laender.
● The head of state is the federal president. He or she represents the country in national matters.
● The federal president is elected for five years by the federal convention.

1
2
Schleswig–Holstein   Hamburg

3
Bremen

4
Lower Saxony

5
Saxony–Anhalt

6
Mecklenburg–West Pomerania

7
North Rhine–Westphalia

8
Berlin

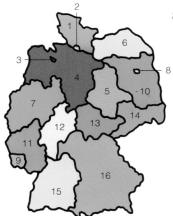

9
Saarland

10
Brandenburg

11
Rhineland–Palatinate

12
Hesse

13
Thuringia

14
Saxony

15
Baden–Württemberg

16
Bavaria

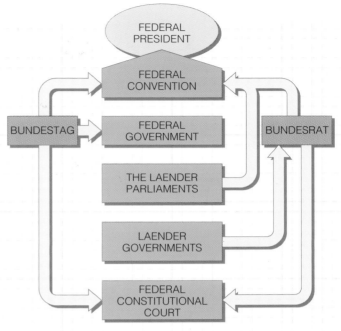

FEDERAL PRESIDENT

FEDERAL CONVENTION

BUNDESTAG

FEDERAL GOVERNMENT

BUNDESRAT

THE LAENDER PARLIAMENTS

LAENDER GOVERNMENTS

FEDERAL CONSTITUTIONAL COURT

Head of state is the federal president, elected for 5 years by the federal convention.

The federal convention is made up of all members of the Bundestag and an equal number of members elected by the Laender parliaments.

▲*The number of seats in the Bundestag had to be increased from 519 to 663 in 1990 when the country was reunified. The Bundestag moved from Bonn to its new home in Berlin.*

▼*The German armed forces are part of NATO (North Atlantic Treaty Organization) which includes the U.S., U.K., and other European countries.*

The chief political parties are the Christian Democratic Union (CDU), the Social Democratic Party (SPD), and the Free Democratic Party (FDP). To have any seats in the Bundestag a political party must win five percent of the votes throughout the country. This is hard on small parties like the ecological Green Party.

The head of state is the federal president but he or she has little political power. The real power is held by the chancellor, who is elected by the members of the Bundestag at the suggestion of the federal president. In practice, the chancellor is the head of the party that has won most votes in the election. The chancellor appoints the ministers of government.

The Federal Constitutional Court is the highest court in Germany. It deals with disputes between the central government and the Laender.

FOOD AND FARMING

In the west and south of Germany farms are small, covering between 64 and 124 acres (25 and 50 ha). Despite this, the farms are highly efficient, with the result that Germany produces 75 percent of its own food. There are still some of the traditional tiny German farms of less than 25 acres (10 ha). Most of these are worked part-time by people who also have another job. Overall, 65 percent of all farmers have a second job.

In the eastern regions the large state and COLLECTIVE FARMS used to be owned by the government. These are being broken up into smaller units, and sold to cooperative groups of farmers. In the past the government in these eastern areas dictated what crops to grow and which animals to keep. Now individual farmers and FARMING COOPERATIVES are free to decide for themselves.

The cool, damp conditions throughout most of Germany encourage the growth of grass for DAIRY FARMING or grains, such as wheat and barley, for ARABLE FARMING. In the cool, wet part of northern Germany rye and oats used to be important crops. Today, however, fewer farmers grow them because plant breeders have developed types of wheat and barley that will thrive in the more northern areas, and both of these crops are more useful than oats and rye. Sugar beets and grains are grown on the plains and lowlands of northern Germany as food for cattle, which are reared for their milk and meat.

In southern Germany the hotter summers mean that corn can be grown as feed for cattle and pigs. Most pigs are reared on factory farms to meet the large demand for pork and *Wurst* (sausages). Pig rearing has increased by 40 percent in the last 10 years.

Grapes are an important crop on sunny, south-facing slopes in the Rhine and Moselle valleys. Steep hillsides are terraced to create flat land for the vines. Traditionally, Rhine wine is sold in brown bottles and Moselle in green ones.

FARM SIZES IN ACRES (ha)
1970 and 1980 figures for W. Germany

1970

over 50 (20 ha) | 12–50 (5–20 ha)

16.4 | 46.2
14.3
23.1

2.5–5 (1–2 ha) | 5–12 (2–5 ha)
Total 48,066 (19,460 ha)

1980

26.3 | 41.7
12.9
19.1

Total 44,882 (18,171 ha)

1990
(United Germany)

45.1
10.1 | 30.6
14.2

Total 43,773 (17,722 ha)

◀ West Germany was a country of small farms while East Germany had large state-owned farms. Now many small farms are being joined together.

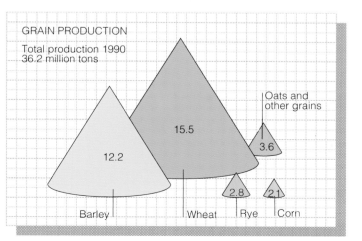

GRAIN PRODUCTION
Total production 1990
36.2 million tons

Barley 12.2
Wheat 15.5
Oats and other grains 3.6
Rye 2.8
Corn 2.1

◀ Wheat is Germany's main grain crop and production is increasing. Much of the wheat is made into flour. Barley is mostly used for brewing beer or converting into animal feed.

PRODUCTION OF GRAINS IN THE U.S., EC, AND JAPAN, 1990 (million tons)				
	Wheat	Barley	Oats	Corn
Germany	15.5	12.2	3.6	2.1
Belgium	1.3	0.8	0.08	0.06
Denmark	2.3	5.4	0.1	–
Greece	2.5	0.7	0.07	2.3
Spain	6.2	10.8	0.6	4
France	30.6	11.2	1.5	14.1
Ireland	0.4	1.7	0.1	–
Italy	9.8	1.8	0.3	6.8
Luxembourg	0.03	0.07	0.2	–
Netherlands	0.9	0.02	0.06	–
Portugal	0.6	0.08	0.14	0.7
U.K.	13.8	10.23	0.6	0.04
EC	83.93	55	7.35	30.10
U.S.	59.8	11.4	5.8	188.5
Japan	1.1	0.3	–	–

▲ *This combine harvester is working in Schleswig-Holstein. Large machines need large fields, so fences and hedges between fields have been removed.*

KEY FACTS

● Only 5 percent of Germans now work in agriculture. In 1960 the figure was 20 percent.

● The number of farms decreased from 2.1 million in 1950 to 650,000 in 1990.

● Germany has more than 23 million pigs, 20 million cattle, and 1.1 million sheep.

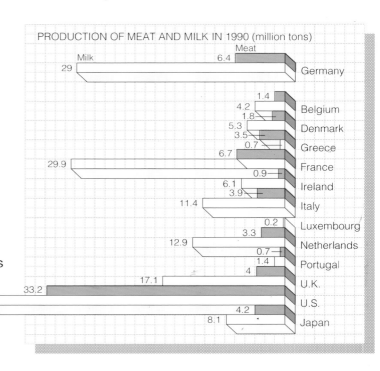

▲ *In modern milking parlors cows get a measured ration of food during milking.*

▼ *Germany and France dominate meat and milk production in the EC.*

German breakfasts usually consist of brown or white rolls with jam, marmalade, butter, coffee, and perhaps a boiled egg or cold meat. Because people have to leave home around 7:30 A.M. for school or work, most take sandwiches and a drink to have in the middle of the morning. Lunch is the most important meal of the day. There is usually a meat dish, with cooked vegetables, potatoes, and gravy. Pork is the most popular meat, followed by veal, chicken, and beef. The evening meal usually consists of a selection of cold meats

PRODUCTION OF MEAT AND MILK IN 1990 (million tons)

	Milk	Meat	
Germany	29	6.4	
Belgium	4.2	1.4	
Denmark	5.3	1.8	
Greece		3.5 / 0.7	
France	29.9	6.7	
Ireland	6.1	0.9	
Italy	11.4	3.9	
Luxembourg		0.2	
Netherlands	12.9	3.3	
Portugal		0.7 / 1.4	
U.K.	17.1	4	
U.S.	71.2	33.2	
Japan	8.1	4.2	

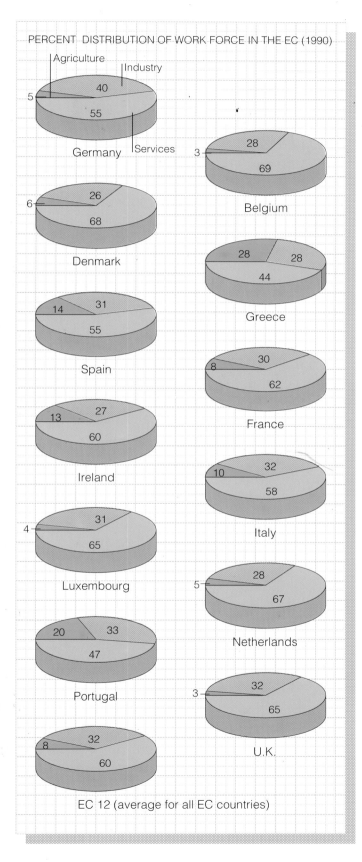

PERCENT DISTRIBUTION OF WORK FORCE IN THE EC (1990)

Agriculture | Industry

Germany | Services
40
55
5

Denmark
26
68
6

Spain
31
14
55

Ireland
27
13
60

Luxembourg
31
65
4

Portugal
33
20
47

EC 12 (average for all EC countries)
32
8
60

Belgium
28
69
3

Greece
28 28
44

France
30
62
8

Italy
32
10
58

Netherlands
28
67
5

U.K.
32
65
3

together with bread, cheese, and fruit.

Sausages are a German specialty, especially the famous frankfurter. Each part of the country has its favorite sausage recipe, and many regions brew their own local beers. These have now become popular in other countries.

The different parts of Germany have become famous for particular types of food. In the north, near the sea, fish dishes with eels and lobsters are popular. In Westphalia, in the northwest, smoked ham is served with pumpernickel, a brown rye bread. Munich is famous for its white sausages. The *enitopf*, or meal in a pot, is popular at noon in Berlin. It is a thick pea or lentil soup with sausage.

◄**The importance of agriculture varies from one country to another within the European Community.**

▲**The Metzgerei or butcher's shop sells a wide range of different types of sausages.**

▲ *Germany's wealth is based on industrial growth. This development in Godorf on the Rhine River is typical of many developments throughout the country.*

KEY FACTS

● Germany is the world's third largest producer of buses and trucks after Japan and the U.S.

● Germany is the world's fifth largest producer of TV sets after Japan, China, the U.S. and Russia.

● Germany is the world's third largest ship-building nation after Japan and South Korea.

● Germany is the world's fourth largest car tire manufacturer after the U.S., Japan, and Russia.

Germany is one of the world's most successful industrial nations. Huge chemical refineries, iron and steel works, engineering and textile factories, and banks and insurance companies have helped to make it a rich, powerful country.

In the 19th century traditional industries such as iron, steel, and engineering developed on coalfields like those in the Ruhr. At this time, Germany's production of steel, ships, railroads, trains, and machines was third only to that of the U.K. and the U.S. These traditional heavy industries developed close to the mines that provided raw materials such as iron ore and fuel in the form of coal. Since 1945, most of the traditional industries have been completely rebuilt with modern factories and machines. More than two million people still work in Germany's heavy industries producing cars,

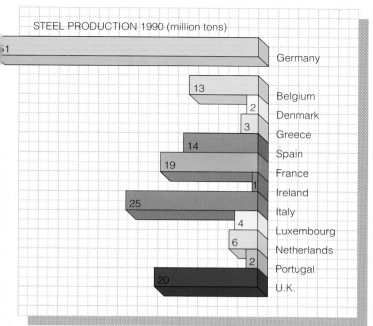

STEEL PRODUCTION 1990 (million tons)

Germany	51
Belgium	13
Denmark	2
Greece	3
Spain	14
France	19
Ireland	1
Italy	25
Luxembourg	4
Netherlands	6
Portugal	2
U.K.	20

▲ *Germany is by far the most important European steel producer.*

▶ *Engineering industries have grown around steelworks in areas like the Ruhr, the most important heavy industrial area in Europe.*

trucks, ships, robots, and a wide range of machines. Many of these goods are exported all over the world as German engineering has an extremely good reputation.

The chemical industry was developed on the lignite (brown coal) fields. But when oil became the basis of the industry, refineries were built along the Rhine and Elbe rivers where the oil could be imported by barge or pipeline. Now the chemical industry produces a huge range of goods from pharmaceuticals to paints, plastics, insecticides, and videotapes.

Many new industries have developed since 1945, producing goods such as musical instruments and video recorders. These factories are not closely linked to either coalfields or rivers but are described as FOOTLOOSE because they can be set up almost anywhere. As a result, a lot of the new factories have been built in southern Germany where there was cheaper land, more space for expansion, and a pleasant, unpolluted ENVIRONMENT. Towns such as Stuttgart, Freiburg, and Munich have all shared in this growth.

Expensive glassware and high quality ceramics are made in both east and south Germany. Almost all towns have workshops that make a variety of goods from toys to clothes.

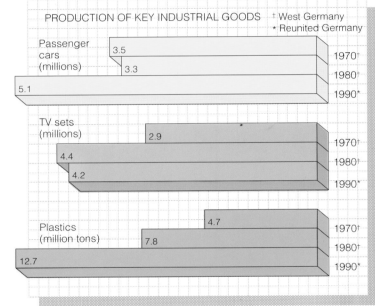

Modern car factories need lots of space, so they are usually built at the edge of a town where land is cheaper and there is the added advantage of nearby main roads and highways.

As the German economy has grown, the country's industrialists have turned to producing new and better products. Consumer goods, such as television sets, washing machines, refrigerators, and microwave ovens, are manufactured close to large cities like Düsseldorf, Stuttgart, Berlin, and Frankfurt. The output of other consumer goods, such as cigarettes, has increased since unification. East Germans were heavy smokers, but health workers hope to reduce the consumption of cigarettes.

Germany also has a reputation for making high-quality, precision goods, like binoculars, cameras, and microscopes. Firms such as Zeiss in Jena are world famous for their optical instruments.

Volkswagen and Mercedes-Benz dominate the German automobile industry. The companies make vans, buses, and trucks as well as cars. The car industry has component factories that each make a particular part, such as transmissions, engines, spark plugs, or axles. These are then taken to the assembly plant and put together on the computer controlled assembly line where robots are used for

PRODUCTION OF KEY INDUSTRIAL GOODS
† West Germany
* Reunited Germany

Passenger cars (millions)		
3.5		1970
3.3		1980
5.1		1990*

TV sets (millions)		
2.9		1970†
4.4		1980†
4.2		1990†

Plastics (million tons)		
4.7		1970†
7.8		1980†
12.7		1990*

KEY FACTS

● In 1990 Germany produced 5.1 million cars.
● Volkswagen, Europe's fourth largest car producer, is based at Wolfsburg near Brunswick.
● Firms in the west of the country are opening branches in the east where wage rates are lower.

many of the tasks. Using robots reduces costs and increases efficiency but can mean fewer jobs and even unemployment for human workers.

After the country was unified in 1990, East German car factories were found to be old and to have inefficient, out-of-date machinery. These factories are now being modernized but the new equipment is expensive, and the modernization is slow. As a result, many former car workers will be out of work for a considerable time.

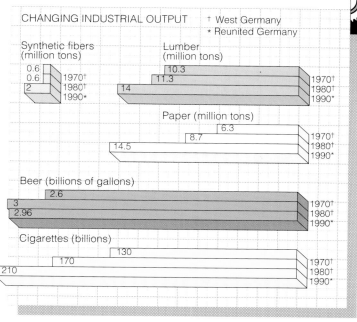

CHANGING INDUSTRIAL OUTPUT   † West Germany
                              * Reunited Germany

Synthetic fibers (million tons)
0.6   1970†
0.6   1980†
2   1990*

Lumber (million tons)
10.3   1970†
11.3   1980†
14   1990*

Paper (million tons)
6.3   1970†
8.7   1980†
14.5   1990*

Beer (billions of gallons)
2.6   1970†
3   1980†
2.96   1990*

Cigarettes (billions)
130   1970†
170   1980†
210   1990*

Germany has a reputation for producing high-quality goods, like this Porsche car. Precision engineering is associated with modern design, styling, and reliability. One of the reasons for Germany's continued success as an exporter of cars and other manufactured goods is its concentration on high-quality, high-value products.

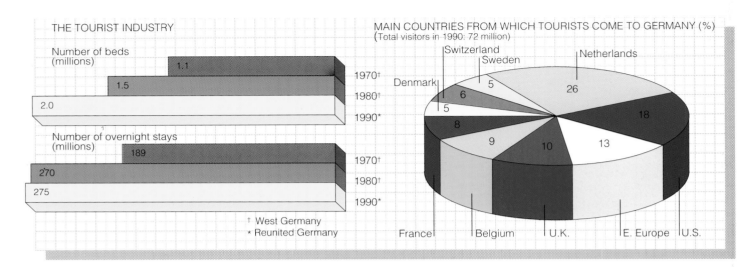

THE TOURIST INDUSTRY

Number of beds
(millions)

1.1	1970†
1.5	1980†
2.0	1990*

Number of overnight stays
(millions)

189	1970†
270	1980†
275	1990*

† West Germany
* Reunited Germany

MAIN COUNTRIES FROM WHICH TOURISTS COME TO GERMANY (%)
(Total visitors in 1990: 72 million)

Switzerland 5
Sweden
Netherlands 26
Denmark 6
5
8
9
10
13
18

France | Belgium | U.K. | E. Europe | U.S.

The tourist industry in Germany is based on three main types of resources:

Natural resources, such as the Alps, the rivers, the beaches, and the climate.

Cultural resources, which are based on the culture of the local people, especially their way of life, including food, festivals, clothes, castles, and dances. Here the traditional regional costumes, such as the *lederhosen* (leather pants), and festivals, like *Oktoberfest,* are important.

Specially-built resources, which include restaurants, hotels, swimming pools, airports, and chair lifts. These have been built to make sure visitors have a good time.

◄ *High-quality porcelain has been made in Dresden since the early 18th century. Porcelain is made by baking clay at very high temperatures. Meissen and Dresden are two of the main centers, famous for their beautiful figures, vases, ornaments, and tableware. Many of the finest pieces are hand-painted by skilled artists.*

KEY FACTS

● The average length of stay in German resorts is 5 days.

● In 1990, 72 million foreign visitors arrived in Germany.

● Some tourist centers, like Berlin or the Zugspitze mountain, attract large numbers of visitors and are called "honey pot" sites.

● Germany offers many city-based vacations (e.g., Munich), beach vacations (e.g., the Baltic coast), forest vacations (e.g., the Black Forest), mountain vacations (e.g., the Alps), and river vacations (e.g., the Rhine and the Elbe).

● More than 18 percent of Germany's work force is employed in financial services.

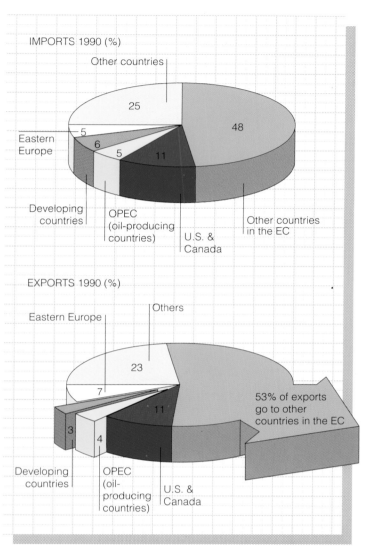

IMPORTS 1990 (%)

Other countries — 25
48
Eastern Europe — 5
6
5
11
Developing countries
OPEC (oil-producing countries)
U.S. & Canada
Other countries in the EC

EXPORTS 1990 (%)

Eastern Europe
Others
23
7
11
3
4
53% of exports go to other countries in the EC
Developing countries
OPEC (oil-producing countries)
U.S. & Canada

Millions of people depend on tourism for their living. Some work in hotels and airports, others in restaurants or as guides or taxi drivers. Farmers close to tourist centers take in visitors and sell some of their food to the tourist hotels. Other people earn a living by making goods, like cameras, food, toys, or binoculars, to sell to the tourists.

Tourism, however, can bring problems as well as wealth. As the number of visitors increases, traffic jams become worse in cities like Cologne and Munich. As a result, air pollution can become a serious problem. There is also the danger that traditional forms of dress, music, and dance will become no more than shows for tourists.

▶ *Every day thousands of stocks and shares are bought and sold on the Frankfurt Stock Exchange. When an economy is growing, stocks and shares increase in value, but their value falls when an economy shrinks.*

▲*Electric streetcars help reduce air pollution in cities like Düsseldorf. These systems are expensive to build but are popular with commuters and shoppers.*

In the 1930s Germany became the first European country to build *autobahnen* (highways). Although much of the network was damaged in 1945 at the end of World War II, the routes have been rebuilt and extended. The *autobahnen* in what was East Germany are being improved to match those in the rest of the country.

The Deutsche Bundesbahn (German railroads) provide a fast, frequent service between the main towns and cities. This is particularly important because Germany is such a big country. The new high-speed train from Berlin to Hanover will cut traveling time by more than 30 percent. New locomotives are faster, heavier, and more powerful, enabling 30 percent of the country's goods traffic to be carried on the railroads.

Underground railroads in Berlin, Hamburg, and Munich are important in getting commuters to and from work. Berlin has two underground subway systems. The S'Bahn is the older of the two and is being modernized and old stations reopened.

Air travel is popular within Germany because of the country's size. Lufthansa, the national airline, has routes to all main cities from its base in Frankfurt. International routes are based in Berlin and Frankfurt.

Pipelines have recently become an important form of transportation. They are especially important for liquids like crude oil.

KEY FACTS

● In 1990 Germany had 27,220 miles (44,090 km) of railroad, 10 percent less than in 1970.
● Thirty-three percent of families in Germany have two cars, and five percent of families have three or more cars.
● Each year Germans spend on average DM1,600 ($1,100) on car repairs.

►*The network of canals and navigable rivers, like the Rhine, carry 25 percent of Germany's goods. "Push" barges like this one can move far heavier loads than traditional "pull" barges.*

INLAND WATERWAYS (1990)

	Length of waterways in use in miles (km)	No. of goods vessels	Tons carried (millions)
Germany	4,213 (6,780)	3,564	341.1
Belgium	941 (1,514)	2,214	100
France	3,121 (5,023)	4,565	62.5
Netherlands	3,002 (4,831)	3,019	264.7
U.S.	10,000 (16,093)	38,000	606

CIVIL AVIATION (1990)

	Number of airlines	Number of aircraft	Passenger miles (km) (millions)
Germany	1	305	20,380 (32,797)
Belgium	1	70	3,712 (5,973)
Denmark	2	97	2,073 (3,336)
Greece	1	44	4,425 (7,121)
Spain	1	197	12,681 (20,408)
France	2	461	23,040 (37,079)
Ireland	1	55	345 (555)
Italy	1	180	9,535 (15,344)
Netherlands	1	128	13,568 (21,835)
Portugal	1	45	3,692 (4,976)
U.K.	2	729	28,741 (46,253)
U.S.	64	4,017	454,300 (731,105)

▲ *Waterways are important for moving goods around Europe, but air transportation is vital for the movement of people.*

Germans recognize the importance of protecting their environment. One of the main environmental threats is from ACID RAIN. Since the 1970s the rain falling on Germany has become more and more acidic. All rain contains some acid because the water dissolves gases in the air like sulfur dioxide. Recently, however, the amount of sulfur dioxide in the air has increased. In turn this has made the rain more acidic. Acid rain kills fish and plants in rivers and lakes. Trees are damaged or even killed by acid rain, and now half of all the Black Forest trees are affected. Acid rain can be prevented by fitting special filters to power stations. The filters remove the sulfur dioxide, but they are also very expensive.

Germany's rivers and lakes are polluted by waste from farms, factories, and towns. Chemicals used to control insects or weeds on farms find their way into the water system. When this happens, plants, fish, and wildlife die. Despite stricter laws, factories still

▲*Many farmers spray chemicals such as pesticides and artificial fertilizers from the air. Only about 20 percent of the spray lands on the crops, the rest may be blown away and affect the lungs of people living nearby.*

▶*Polluted water from a phosphate factory is discharged into the river. Industrial waste can be very toxic, especially that containing heavy metals like cadmium and lead, as well as liquids such as cyanide.*

sometimes pollute water supplies. Some sewage and domestic waste from towns along the Elbe River also gets into the rivers.

One of the most recent threats to the environment is the growing use by industry of strong cleaning fluids. These fluids are called polychlorinated biphenyls, or PCBs for short, and have become important in factories. However, when they escape into

KEY FACTS

● In 1990, Germany produced 326,700 tons of pesticides and herbicides.

● In the forests of the Harz mountains some rare animals, like the lynx and the wildcat, still manage to survive.

● The golden eagle has begun to breed again in the alpine areas of southern Germany.

● Some power stations have special incinerators to burn domestic garbage to generate electricity for local apartments.

● Some buildings are losing 4 percent of their weight each year as acid rain eats away the brick and stone.

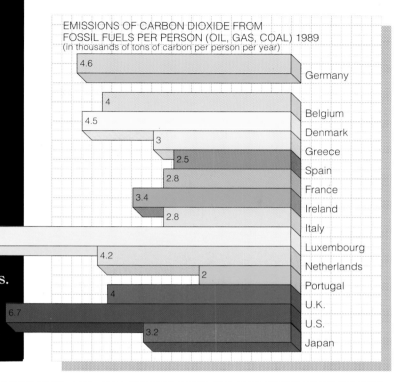

EMISSIONS OF CARBON DIOXIDE FROM FOSSIL FUELS PER PERSON (OIL, GAS, COAL) 1989
(in thousands of tons of carbon per person per year)

Germany	4.6
Belgium	4
Denmark	4.5
Greece	3
Spain	2.5
France	2.8
Ireland	3.4
Italy	2.8
Luxembourg	8.1
Netherlands	4.2
Portugal	2
U.K.	4
U.S.	6.7
Japan	3.2

▲ *German national parks were created to preserve areas of outstanding natural beauty. These areas are protected to prevent the growth of farms, mines, and towns from threatening the existence of wilderness areas. Developments within the parks are carefully controlled, as is the number of visitors.*

rivers and lakes, they kill all forms of life. Germany is now trying to control this type of pollution by imposing heavy fines on firms that fail to treat their waste properly.

Despite these problems, Germany is improving the environment in many areas. In the forests of the east and south, wild boars, adders, and deer continue to multiply. The numbers of chamois, a type of deer, and ibex, a type of goat, are also increasing in the Alps. Species like the eagle owl, Elbe beaver, horseshoe bat, and wildcat, which were all threatened with extinction, now enjoy special protection.

Even within cities, the environment is being improved by projects to redevelop slum areas or to reduce the volume of traffic and increase the area of parks and green space. Cars, trucks, and buses are burning more lead-free gasoline, and special converters fitted to vehicle exhausts are helping to improve air quality. The nuclear power program has been halted because of the fear of an escape of radioactivity. Instead, alternative forms of energy that use wind, water, or sunlight are being developed.

THE FUTURE

Germany only became a united country in 1871. In 1945 it was again divided and reunification did not come until 1990. Despite all these dramatic changes, Germany has become a rich and powerful country whose people enjoy a high standard of living. Because of its size, position, and economic strength Germany has become one of the most important

▼ *Because of advances in modern medicine, many more diseases can be treated or cured, and many more people will live into old age. New techniques, new treatments, and new drugs are being developed as a result of research funded by government and industry.*

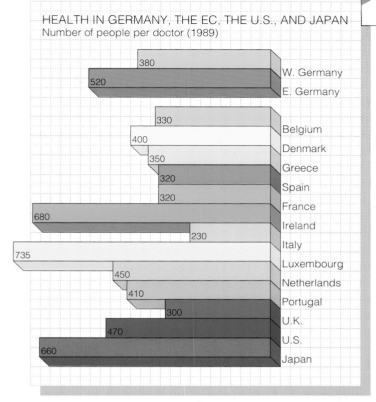

HEALTH IN GERMANY, THE EC, THE U.S., AND JAPAN
Number of people per doctor (1989)

Country	Number of people per doctor
W. Germany	380
E. Germany	520
Belgium	330
Denmark	400
Greece	350
Spain	320
France	320
Ireland	680
Italy	230
Luxembourg	735
Netherlands	450
Portugal	410
U.K.	300
U.S.	470
Japan	660

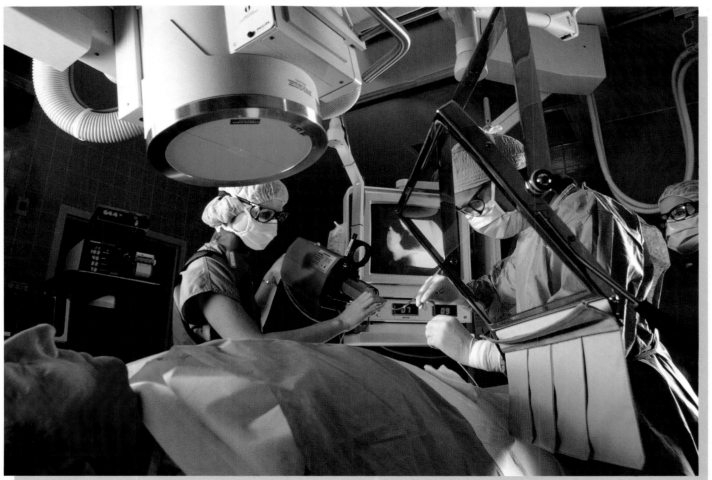

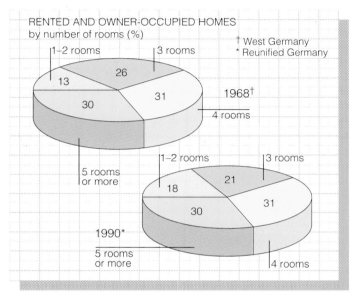

◀ *A new building development in what used to be East Berlin.*

▼ *Since reunification, the number of one-to two-room homes has risen because more East Germans still live in small apartments*

RENTED AND OWNER-OCCUPIED HOMES
by number of rooms (%)

† West Germany
* Reunified Germany

1968†

1–2 rooms 13
3 rooms 26
31
30
4 rooms

1990*

1–2 rooms 18
3 rooms 21
5 rooms or more
30
31
5 rooms or more
4 rooms

members of the European Community. This importance is likely to increase as the EC expands its membership.

Within Germany, much effort has focused on reducing the difference in standards of living between the eastern and western areas. Farms are being modernized, roads rebuilt and factories reequipped in the drive to improve conditions in the east.

Planners are struggling to equalize economic opportunities and incomes in the different regions. Aid is poured into the poorer rural areas in the highlands and parts of the north and east. Nearly half of Germany gets some form of state help.

Between 1945 and 1990, the two parts of Germany were pulled apart. One part was encouraged to look to the West for help, the other to look to the Communist countries in the east. Germany's own identity is only now beginning to emerge since the reunification of the country. The nation's prosperity, its economic strength, and its sense of history will be important factors in the future of both Germany and Europe.

KEY FACTS

● Germany is spending more than DM 300 million ($189 million) to reduce problems of noise near highways and airports.

● More than DM 2 billion ($1.26 billion) are being spent building new roads and railroads in the eastern parts of Germany.

● Funds from the U.S., Canada; Switzerland, and the U.K. are helping to rebuild the eastern parts of Germany.

►*Although Berlin is many miles (km) from the sea, a popular beach has been created around the Wannsee Lake. Here Berliners can relax and improve their suntans yet still be close to their homes and work. In the future people will have more leisure time so other cities will need to build artificial beaches.*

FURTHER INFORMATION

THE GERMAN EMBASSY
4645 Reservoir Road, NW, Washington, D.C. 20007

GERMAN INFORMATION CENTER
410 Park Avenue, New York, NY 10022

GOETHE HOUSE NEW YORK
1014 Fifth Avenue, New York, NY 10028

GERMAN NATIONAL TOURIST OFFICE
747 Third Avenue 33rd Floor, New York, NY 10017

BOOKS ABOUT GERMANY

Adler, Ann. *A Family in West Germany.* Lerner, 1985

Ayer, Eleanor. *Germany.* Rourke Corp., 1990

Bailey, Donna. *Germany.* Raintree Steck-Vaughn, 1992

Garrett, Dan and Drew-Bernstein, Charlotte. *Germany.* Raintree Steck-Vaughn, 1992

Hargrove, Jim. *Germany.* Childrens, 1991

Pfeiffer, Christine. *Germany: Two Nations, One Heritage.* Macmillan Child Grp., 1987

Philpotts, Beatrice. *Germany.* Silver Burdett, 1989

GLOSSARY

ACID RAIN
Rain polluted by gases, such as sulfur dioxide. Acid rain can cause harm to plants, fish, and animals as well as damage to buildings

ARABLE FARMING
Agriculture in which growing crops is the farmer's main source of income

ARBITUR
Examination taken by pupils at 18 who want to enter a university

BUNDESRAT
The upper house of the German parliament

BUNDESTAG
The lower house of the German parliament

COLLECTIVE FARMS
Farms in East Germany that were owned by the state

DAIRY FARMING
Agriculture that concentrates on rearing cattle to produce milk, cream, butter, and cheese

ENVIRONMENT
All of the things that surround people, such as buildings and natural landscape

FARMING COOPERATIVES
System in which farmers join together to share costs

FOOTLOOSE INDUSTRY
Industries that are not tied to using one source of power or raw material, such as coal or iron ore, and therefore can be started in a wide variety of places

FOREIGN WORKERS
People who have moved from one country to another in order to find work

GYMNASIUM
One of the three types of German secondary school. The word means "grammar school." It does not refer to the school's sports facilities

HAUPTSCHULE
One of the three types of secondary school

LAENDER
The 16 states that make up Germany

LANGLAUF
Cross-country skiing; shorter skies enable skiers to trek up and down hills

LIGNITE
Brown coal; it is softer than black coal but will burn to generate heat

OPEC
The Organization of Petroleum Exporting Countries. It consists of most of the world's main oil-producing countries

PESTICIDES
Chemicals used to kill pests that might harm crops

REALSCHULE
One of the three types of secondary school

RENEWABLE ENERGY
Energy based on power sources that will not run out, such as wind, water, and the sun

STRIP MINING
Mining (particularly lignite) from open pits

WEINFEST
Celebration at the end of the grape harvest

INDEX

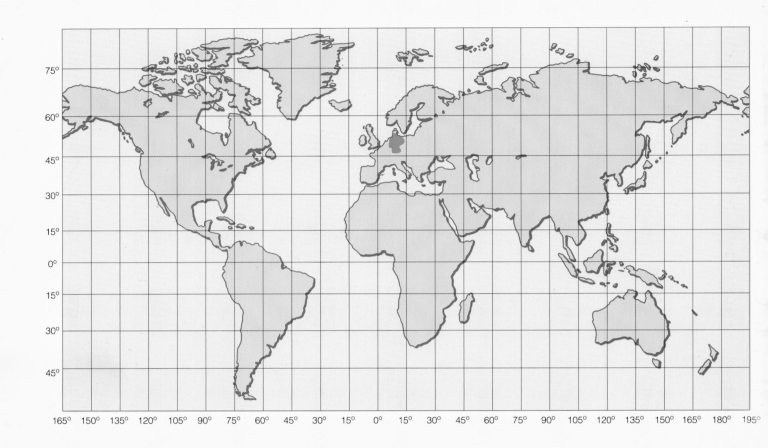